So What?

The Fun and Easy Guide to Handling Workplace Chaos

Copyright © 2024 Maggie Maitriborirak.

All rights reserved.

No part of this publication may be reproduced, distributed, or transmitted in any form or by any means, including photocopying, recording, or other electronic or mechanical methods, without prior written permission from the author, except for brief quotations in a book review, journal, or educational context, in compliance with copyright law. For permissions, inquiries, or additional rights requests, please contact the author at

Maggie.Maitriborirak.oba@said.oxford.edu

This work is registered with all applicable intellectual property protections.

Disclaimer:

The scenarios, characters, and situations presented in this book are purely fictional and are not intended to refer to or depict any specific person, workplace, or event. Any resemblance to actual persons, living or dead, or to any real-life situations is purely coincidental. The content is meant to provide general guidance and humor around common workplace challenges and should be taken as illustrative rather than factual. The lessons shared are meant to offer insight and inspiration, not to target or reference any individual or any organization.

Dedication to My Dad

For every word you never said,
yet every lesson clear,

Your quiet strength, your steady
hand, always drawing near.

Through every trial, every test, your
wisdom showed the way,

In silence, you spoke volumes,
shaping who I am today.

Though you never sought the spotlight,
nor asked for any praise,

Your actions spoke in countless ways,
through all my growing days.

Your love was in the guidance, in
moments calm and true,

This book, this journey, all of it—

Is thanks to you.

Table of Content

Introduction 13
Chapter 1: The Botched Presentation 15
Chapter 2: The Messy Desk 16
Chapter 3: The Last Donut Dilemma 17
Chapter 4: Overthinking the Obvious 19
Chapter 5: The Good-Looking Colleague 20
Chapter 6: The Broken Coffee Machine 21
Chapter 7: The Shared Snacks Sabotage 22
Chapter 8: The Overlooked Idea 23
Chapter 9: The Difficult Client 24
Chapter 10: The Noisy Coworker 25
Chapter 11: The Miscommunication 26
Chapter 12: The Unfair Criticism 27
Chapter 13: The Overload 28
Chapter 14: The Awkward Silence 29
Chapter 15: The "Can You Hear Me?" Chorus 30
Chapter 16: The Odd One Out Adventure 31
Chapter 17: The Rejected Proposal 32
Chapter 18: The Boss Pleaser Olympics 33
Chapter 19: The Missed Promotion 34
Chapter 20: The Forgotten Birthday 35

Chapter 21: The Wrong Email 36
Chapter 22: The Awkward Small Talk 37
Chapter 23: The Missed Deadline 38
Chapter 24: The Unanswered Email 39
Chapter 25: The Decision-Making Ninja......................... 40
Chapter 26: Reading Between the Lines 41
Chapter 27: The Last-Minute Meeting 42
Chapter 28: The Office Party Fumble 43
Chapter 29: The Misjudged Dress Code 44
Chapter 30: The Tough Feedback.................................... 45
Chapter 31: The Monday Blues 46
Chapter 32: The Desk Lunch 47
Chapter 33: The Loud Meeting Room............................. 48
Chapter 34: The Forgotten Password 49
Chapter 35: Playing Office Chess, Not Checkers.............50
Chapter 36: The Casual Friday Confusion 52
Chapter 37: The Overbooked Calendar 53
Chapter 38: The Undercover Leader 54
Chapter 39: The Forgotten Meeting 56
Chapter 40: The Copycat Colleague 57
Chapter 41: The "No Alcohol" Commitment in a Sea of Happy Hour Enthusiasts 58
Chapter 42: The Late Arrival... 59
Chapter 43: The Overslept Alarm 60
Chapter 44: The Performance Review Panic 61
Chapter 45: The Empathy Jedi... 62
Chapter 46: The Emoji Overload 63

Chapter 47: The "Forgot the Attachment" Fumble 64
Chapter 48: Zoom Background Bluff 65
Chapter 49: The Mentorship Maze 66
Chapter 50: The Guilt Tug-of-War 67
Chapter 51: The "Am I Allowed to Be Proud?" Dilemma 68
Chapter 52: The Green-Eyed You Monster 69
Chapter 53: The Last-Minute Project 70
Chapter 54: The Critical Email 71
Chapter 55: The Budget Cuts 72
Chapter 56: The Out-of-Touch Boss 73
Chapter 57: The Networking Nightmare 74
Chapter 58: The Presentation Interruptions 75
Chapter 59: The Forgotten File 76
Chapter 60: The Conference Call Fail 77
Chapter 61: The Client Ghosting 78
Chapter 62: The Working Weekend 79
Chapter 63: The Over Enthusiastic Team Member 80
Chapter 64: The Silent Treatment 81
Chapter 65: The Introvert's Survival Challenge 82
Chapter 66: The Salary Expectation vs. Reality Show 83
Chapter 67: The Work-Life Balance Sweet Spot 84
Chapter 68: The Favoritism Fiasco 85
Chapter 69: The Colleague Competition Showdown 86
Chapter 70: The Knowledge Sponge 2.0 87
Chapter 71: The Integrity Ninja 88
Chapter 72: The Feedback Dance-Off 89
Chapter 73: The Avengers Assemble Moment 90

Chapter 74: The MacGyver Moment 91
Chapter 75: The Exit Interview 92
Chapter 76: The Overbooked Travel Schedule 93
Chapter 77: The Copy Machine Conundrum 94
Chapter 78: The Morning Coffee Spill 95
Chapter 79: The Forgetful Colleague 96
Chapter 80: The Office Fridge Fiasco 97
Chapter 81: The Micromanaging Boss 98
Chapter 82: The Elevator Pitch Gone Wrong 99
Chapter 83: The Broken Chair Incident 100
Chapter 84: The Surprise Office Visit .... 101 **Chapter 85:** The Delayed Feedback .... 102 **Chapter 86:** The Conference Room Double-Booking .... 103 **Chapter 87:** The Chatty Co-Worker .... 104 **Chapter 88:** The Misunderstood comment .... 105 **Chapter 89:** The Endless Conference Call .... 106 **Chapter 90:** The Unreturned Call .... 107 **Chapter 91:** The No-Show Interviewee .... 108 **Chapter 92:** The Overlapping Deadlines .... 109 **Chapter 93:** The Confusing Office Jargon .... 110 **Chapter 94:** The Silent Office Party .... 111 **Chapter 95:** The Overly Complicated Password Policy 112
Chapter 96: The Meeting That Could Have Been an Email 113
Chapter 97: The Tech Glitch Disaster 114
Chapter 98: The Office Rivalry .... 115 **Chapter 99:** The Oversharing Colleague 116

Chapter 100: The "What Do You Think About Them?" Colleague 117

Chapter 101: The Group Project Dilemma 118

Chapter 102: The Mystery Meeting Invitation 119

Chapter 103: The Messy Whiteboard 120

Chapter 104: The Unexpected Office Fire Drill 121

Chapter 105: The Broken Printer 122

Chapter 106: The Disastrous First Day 123

Chapter 107: The Team Outing Gone Wrong 124

Chapter 108: The Unreliable Wi-Fi 125

Chapter 109: The Last-Minute Client Request 126

Chapter 110: The Holiday Work Rush 127

Chapter 111: The Unrealistic Deadline 128

Chapter 112: The Inconsistent Policies 129

Chapter 113: The Missed Opportunity 130

Chapter 114: The Never-Ending To-Do List 131

Chapter 115: The Lost Key Card 132

Chapter 116: The Office Temperature Battle 133

Chapter 117: The Loud Typist 134

Chapter 118: The Printer Paper Jam 135

Chapter 119: The Unread Newsletter 136

Chapter 120: The Forgotten Phone Charger 137

Chapter 121: The Inbox Full of Spam 138

Chapter 122: The Misspelled Name 139

Chapter 123: The Overly Complex Spreadsheet 140

Chapter 124: The Office Microwave Meltdown 141

Chapter 125: The Mr./Miss Know-It-All Showdown 142

Chapter 126: The Team "Too Many Cooks" Moment.........143
Chapter 127: The Micro-Aggression Moment...................144
Chapter 128: The Boss Who's All Talk, No Action 145
Chapter 129: The Technology Takeover..........................146
Chapter 130: The Team That Missed the Mark.................147
Chapter 131: The Silent Power Struggle..........................148
Chapter 132: The "I Forgot the Time Zone" Mix-Up..........149
Chapter 133: The Boss Who Changes Their Mind 150
Chapter 134: The "Wrong Zoom Room" Fiasco 151
Chapter 135: The Subordinate with Big Ideas 152
Chapter 136: The Office Gossip Gauntlet 153
Chapter 137: The Subtle Sabotage................................154
Chapter 138: The "We Don't Know What We're Doing" Project..155
Chapter 139: The Boss Who Can't Let Go 156
Chapter 140: The Values Clash 157
Chapter 141: The "Is This Really My Job?" Moment..........158
Chapter 142: The Last-Minute Presentation Hero 159
Chapter 143: The "Forgot My Pants" Dream 160
Chapter 144: The Too Many Buzzwords Meeting 161
Chapter 145: The All-Day Meeting Marathon 162
Chapter 146: The "What Was My Point Again?" 163
Chapter 147: The Never-Ending Spreadsheet...................164
Chapter 148: The Epic IT Fail 165
Chapter 149: The Email Typos You Missed 166
Chapter 150: The "Can't Stop Laughing" Meeting 167
Chapter 151: The End-of-Day Energy Crash....................168

Chapter 152: The "Do It My Way" Colleague 169
Chapter 153: The Return from Vacation Overload 170
Chapter 154: The Never-Ending Notifications 171
Chapter 155: The Rogue Autocorrect 172
Chapter 156: The Boss's Unclear Instructions 173
Chapter 157: The "I Forgot My Password Again" Day 174
Chapter 158: The Personal Errand at Work 175
Chapter 159: The Misinterpreted Email Tone 176
Chapter 160: The Printer Paper Panic 177
Chapter 161: The Office Party Mishap 178
Chapter 162: The Working Lunch Confusion 179
Chapter 163: The Imposter Syndrome Attack 180
Chapter 164: The Rare Boss Compliment 181
Chapter 165: The Unexpected Work Travel..................... 182
Chapter 166: The "Forgot My Presentation" Nightmare.... 183
Chapter 167: The "Let's Circle Back" Loop 184
Chapter 168: The "That's Not My Job" Colleague 185
Chapter 170: The One Who Forgets Your Name 186
Chapter 171: The Office Group Chat Explosion 187
Chapter 172: The Professional Juggler 188
Chapter 173: The Over-Organized Desk 189
Chapter 174: The Office Plant Obsession 190
Chapter 175: The Neverending Training Session............. 191
Chapter 176: The Colleague with the Best Snacks 192
Chapter 177: The Colleague Who Lights Up the Room 193
Chapter 178: The Unexpected Mentor 194
Chapter 179: The Power of Listening 195

Chapter 180: The Surprising Source of Inspiration 196
Chapter 181: The Coffee Shop "Influencer" 197
Chapter 182: The Surprise Desk Gift 198
Chapter 183: The "One More Thing" Boss 199
Chapter 184: The Unplanned Office Dance Party 200
Chapter 185: The Last-Minute Team Save........................201
Chapter 186: The Free Office Lunch Surprise 202
Chapter 187: The "Random Compliment" Day 203
Chapter 188: The Office Prank (That's Actually Fun) 204
Chapter 189: The Snow Day Surprise 205
Chapter 190: The Impromptu Birthday Celebration 206
Chapter 191: The Friendly Office Competitions 207
Chapter 192: The "Pay It Forward" Moment 208
Chapter 193: The Colleague Who Always Has Your Back..209
Chapter 194: The "Forgot My Glasses" Presentation 210
Chapter 195: The Overly Ambitious Lunch Choice 211
Chapter 196: The Accidental Screen Share 212
Chapter 197: The Coffee Cup Identity Crisis 213
Chapter 198: The "Can I Pick Your Brain?" Trap 214
Chapter 199: The Unexpected Promotion Celebration......215
Chapter 200: The "So What?" Moment 216
About the Author 218

INTRODUCTION
Welcome to the Land of Workplace Chaos (and How to Keep Your Cool)

Have you ever had one of those days where everything at work seems to go wrong, and you just want to throw your hands in the air and yell, "Seriously?!" Maybe your presentation crashes, your email gets ignored, or you spill coffee all over your shirt right before that big meeting. And don't even get me started on the awkward Office parties or the printer that seems to break only when you need it most.

But here's the thing: so what?

Yep, you heard me right. So. What.

In this book, we're diving headfirst into the glorious mess that is Office life—filled with drama, mishaps, and all the little things that make you wonder if the universe is playing a prank on you. And we're going to laugh at it. Because at the end of the day, none of those crazy moments define who you are.

So What is your personal guide to brushing off the everyday nonsense of work life with a smile, a shrug, and maybe even a chuckle. It's packed with 200 short, fun chapters covering everything from technical malfunctions to awkward elevator encounters, and yes, even working with that ridiculously good-looking colleague. Each chapter is designed to remind you that no matter how messy things get, you're in control of how you respond.

This book isn't about teaching you how to avoid workplace drama—it's about embracing it with humor and grace. You'll discover how to stay cool, calm, and unflustered, even when the Office coffee machine decides to quit on you. We'll look at all those pesky workplace challenges and say, "So what?"

So grab your favorite mug (preferably one without a coffee stain), take a deep breath, and get ready to laugh your way through the chaos. Because in the end, work is just work. And you? You're so much more.

Here's to keeping it cool,

Maggie Maitriborirak

CHAPTER 1
The Botched Presentation

Scenario: You're presenting to the big bosses, and halfway through, your computer breaks down, and your slides won't load. You panic, stammer a little, and everything feels awkward.

So What?: Technology fails. You didn't. You stayed composed, worked with what you had, and made it through. Your ideas still count, even without the fancy slides. Next time, you'll have an extra story to tell about how you rocked a meeting despite the glitches.

Lesson: It's not the presentation that defines you, it's how you handle the hiccups. Slides can wait; your talent can't.

CHAPTER 2
The Messy Desk

Scenario: Your desk looks like a tornado hit it, and you're embarrassed when someone stops by.

So What?: A messy desk is a sign of a busy mind. You can organize it later, but for now, embrace the creative chaos.

Lesson: It's what comes out of your work that matters, not the state of your desk.

CHAPTER 3
The Last Donut Dilemma

Scenario: It's team lunch, and the table is littered with crumbs and empty plates. All that remains is one solitary donut, sitting there like a beacon of sugary temptation. You can feel the tension in the room. Everyone wants it, but no one wants to be *that person* who grabs it. Eyes dart back and forth, and polite conversation continues, but make no mistake: the real game is waiting for someone to break and reach for the last donut.

So What?: This is a classic workplace showdown of politeness versus desire. You could wait it out, pretending you're not interested, hoping someone else will make the first move. Or, you could be bold, break the tension, and offer to split it! Nothing says "team player" like suggesting a shared donut experience—plus, you get to avoid being *the one* who takes the last bite solo.

Lesson: The Last Donut Dilemma is a delicate balance of workplace etiquette and hunger. Be considerate, but don't deny yourself the simple joys of life (like a good donut). And remember, sometimes the best solution is to just go for it and turn the moment into a fun, team-building snack break. After all, in the end, it's just a donut—don't overthink it!

CHAPTER 4
Overthinking the Obvious

Scenario: Your boss says, "Let's revisit this project later," and you spend hours dissecting what they really meant. Does "later" mean tomorrow, next week, or never? You're analyzing every word like it's a secret code, while your colleagues seem completely unfazed—maybe they actually meant exactly what they said.

So What?: Not every comment is a puzzle to solve. If your boss says, "Let's revisit this later," they probably mean just that—no hidden agendas. Try taking things at face value; it's much less stressful.

Lesson: Overthinking simple statements leads straight to Stressville. Most people mean what they say. Sometimes "later" really just means later. Save the overanalyzing for when it truly matters.

CHAPTER 5
The Good-Looking Colleague

Scenario: You've got a ridiculously good-looking colleague, and sometimes it's hard not to get distracted or flustered during meetings or conversations.

So What?: At the end of the day, looks don't define professionalism, and neither should they affect yours. Keep it cool, focus on the work, and remind yourself that everyone's there for the same reason: to get the job done. Sure, they might be easy on the eyes, but your focus is your superpower. You've got this!

Lesson: Looks fade, but your professionalism and skills are what truly shine. Stay focused on the task at hand, and let your expertise and confidence steal the show.

CHAPTER 6
The Broken Coffee Machine

Scenario: The coffee machine breaks down on a busy Monday morning.

So What?: It's not the end of the world! Grab something else to keep you going—you've got energy to spare.

Lesson: Coffee doesn't power you, your mindset does.

CHAPTER 7
The Shared Snacks Sabotage

Scenario: You're committed to healthy eating, but every time you walk into the break room, there's another birthday cake staring at you. Your apple slices seem sad in comparison to that frosting.

So What?: Stay strong! It's okay to enjoy an occasional treat, but stick to your healthy plan most of the time. Or start a "Healthy Snack Day" to balance the cake overload.

Lesson: Office life is full of sugary temptations, but balance is key. Enjoy the cake now and then, but don't let it derail your goals. Your apple slices will be waiting tomorrow.

CHAPTER 8
The Overlooked Idea

Scenario: You pitch a brilliant idea in a meeting, but no one seems to notice.

So What?: Not every idea gets the spotlight the first time around. Keep bringing your A-game, and people will take notice eventually.

Lesson: Persistence pays off. Great ideas don't fade just because they're ignored at first.

CHAPTER 9
The Dificult Client

Scenario: A client is being unreasonably demanding and borderline rude.

So What?: Their bad attitude doesn't need to become your bad day. Stay calm, set boundaries, and keep your professionalism intact.

Lesson: You can't control others, but you can control how you respond to them.

CHAPTER 10
The Noisy Coworker

Scenario: Your coworker won't stop talking, and you can't focus.

So What?: Distractions happen. Pop in your headphones, politely excuse yourself, or find a quieter spot.

Lesson: You control your environment more than you think. A little creativity can create peace in the chaos.

CHAPTER 11
The Miscommunication

Scenario: A misunderstanding with a colleague creates confusion on a project.

So What?: Miscommunications happen. Clear it up, learn from it, and move on.

Lesson: Communication is a skill, not a one-time event. Clarify and keep the wheels turning.

CHAPTER 12
The Unfair Criticism

Scenario: Your boss gives you criticism that doesn't feel justified.

So What?: Not all feedback will feel fair, but it's still an opportunity to reflect. Take what's helpful, ignore the rest, and keep moving forward.

Lesson: Criticism doesn't define you—your growth does. Filter what you can use and leave the rest behind.

CHAPTER 13
The Overload

Scenario: You've been given more work than you can possibly handle.

So What?: You're not a superhero, and it's okay to ask for help or set boundaries. Prioritize, delegate, and pace yourself.

Lesson: Your capacity has limits, and it's okay to honor them. Pushing back isn't a weakness, it's wisdom.

CHAPTER 14
The Awkward Silence

Scenario: You crack a joke in a meeting, and no one laughs.

So What?: Not every joke lands, but you're not a stand-up comedian. You're here to work, and humor is just a bonus.

Lesson: Awkward moments pass quickly. You're here for more than a punchline.

CHAPTER 15
The "Can You Hear Me?" Chorus

Scenario: You're in a virtual meeting, and suddenly, everything freezes. The dreaded chorus begins: "Can you hear me? Hello? Can you hear me now?" Chaos ensues as everyone taps their mics and repeats the same question, hoping the tech gods will cooperate.

So What?: Smile, give a thumbs-up when sound returns, and silently enjoy the irony of technology making life "easier." While they're stuck in the loop, grab a snack or check your email.

Lesson: Technical glitches are inevitable, but they pass. Stay patient, and soon enough, you'll be back to muted microphones and awkward pauses.

CHAPTER 16
The Odd One Out Adventure

Scenario: You walk into the Office and quickly realize you're the odd one out—whether it's your background, age, or preferences, you just don't seem to fit the mold.

So What?: Embrace it! Your uniqueness brings a fresh perspective, and that's your secret power. Standing out is way more fun than blending in, and often makes you the most memorable person on the team.

Lesson: Don't hide your differences—own them. Being the odd one out is what makes you valuable, helping your team grow and innovate in ways they hadn't imagined.

CHAPTER 17
The Rejected Proposal

Scenario: Your well-thought-out project proposal gets turned down.

So What?: Rejections are part of the game. Time to refine, adapt, and try again.

Lesson: Rejection is redirection. Every "no" leads you closer to a better "yes."

CHAPTER 18
The Boss Pleaser Olympics

Scenario: Your boss mentions liking green tea, and the next day you show up with three types. They praise a colleague for being proactive, and suddenly you're volunteering for every task—big or small. You've become the ultimate boss pleaser.

So What?: It's great to impress your boss, but there's a line between being helpful and becoming the Office "yes person." Instead of trying too hard, let your work speak for itself.

Lesson: Pleasing the boss doesn't require sacrificing your sanity. Focus on quality work, stay cool, and trust that your consistent effort will shine more than endless favors.

CHAPTER 19
The Missed Promotion

Scenario: You worked tirelessly for years, only to watch someone else get the promotion you had your eye on. Ouch, right?

So What?: You didn't lose out; you gained insight. Now you know what's valued in the company, and you have more tools to sharpen. Your time will come, and when it does, you'll be even better prepared to knock it out of the park.

Lesson: One promotion doesn't define your worth. Your growth does. Promotions are stepping stones, not identity markers.

CHAPTER 20
The Forgotten Birthday

Scenario: You forgot a colleague's birthday, and now it's awkward.

So What?: Birthdays happen every year. A quick apology and a small gesture can smooth things over.

Lesson: Relationships matter more than small slip-ups. People remember how you make them feel long after they forget the date.

CHAPTER 21
The Wrong Email

Scenario: You sent an important email to the wrong person.

So What?: Mistakes happen. Follow up with the right person and send a correction if needed. Everyone makes a misstep now and then.

Lesson: A quick recovery is better than dwelling on the mistake. People appreciate eficiency more than perfection.

CHAPTER 22
The Awkward Small Talk

Scenario: You tried to make small talk in the elevator, and it fell flat.

So What?: Not every conversation is a win. Next time, just keep it simple and relaxed.

Lesson: Silence isn't awkward unless you make it so. Let things flow naturally.

CHAPTER 23
The Missed Deadline

Scenario: You missed an important deadline, and now you're scrambling.

So What?: Deadlines can be extended. Communicate with the team, adjust, and focus on delivering quality work.

Lesson: It's better to deliver good work a little late than to rush and submit something half-baked.

CHAPTER 24
The Unanswered Email

Scenario: You sent an important email, but no one responded.

So What?: People get busy, and inboxes overflow. Send a polite follow-up and don't take it personally.

Lesson: Persistence is key. If it's important, keep at it, but don't sweat the silence.

CHAPTER 25
The Decision-Making Ninja

Scenario: You're asked to make a big decision on the spot—no time for meetings, just action.

So What?: Stay calm, slice through the options like a ninja, and choose the best path forward without overthinking.

Lesson: Sometimes, a fast, decisive move is better than endless contemplation. Your confidence and agility are what matter most.

CHAPTER 26
Reading Between the Lines

Scenario: You receive an email from a colleague from another culture saying, "This looks interesting" or "Let's keep this in mind for the future." It sounds positive, but you can't help wondering if they're politely shelving the idea or saying it's not a priority right now. What seems like a simple message could actually be a gentle way of saying, "Not now, maybe never."

So What?: Time to channel your inner Sherlock Holmes. In cross-cultural communication, indirect language can be a way to avoid confrontation or saying no outright. It's important to read between the lines, but it's equally important to ask questions to clarify their true intentions. A simple follow-up like, "Can we revisit this next month?" can help clear up any ambiguity.

Lesson: In cross-cultural communication, subtlety is common. Don't assume—ask for clarification if something sounds vague. Open questions can prevent misunderstandings and make sure you're both on the same page.

CHAPTER 27
The Last-Minute Meeting

Scenario: You're thrown into a last-minute meeting with no time to prepare.

So What?: You're adaptable and quick on your feet. Improvise and trust in your abilities.

Lesson: Sometimes being prepared means being ready for anything, not everything.

CHAPTER 28
The Office Party Fumble

Scenario: You trip and spill your drink at the Office party.

So What?: Everyone loves a good laugh, especially when you can laugh at yourself. Shake it off and enjoy the party.

Lesson: A little clumsiness adds character. It's how you recover that people remember.

CHAPTER 29
The Misjudged Dress Code

Scenario: You show up dressed casually on a day when everyone else is in formal attire.

So What?: Confidence is your best outfit. Own it, and no one will notice the difference.

Lesson: It's not what you wear, but how you carry yourself that makes an impression.

CHAPTER 30
The Tough Feedback

Scenario: You received feedback that stung, and it's hard to take.

So What?: Feedback helps you grow. Take a deep breath, process it, and use it to improve.

Lesson: Growth comes from discomfort. Every piece of feedback is a step toward becoming better.

CHAPTER 31
The Monday Blues

Scenario: It's Monday, and you're struggling to get back into the work groove.

So What?: Mondays come and go. Push through, and by tomorrow, you'll be back on track.

Lesson: The start of the week is just another day. Power through it, and the rest of the week will feel smoother.

CHAPTER 32
The Desk Lunch

Scenario: You're stuck eating lunch at your desk while everyone else is out having fun.

So What?: Sometimes work takes priority, but there's always another opportunity to join the fun.

Lesson: Balance is key. Sometimes it's okay to sacrifice a break, but remember to recharge later.

CHAPTER 33
The Loud Meeting Room

Scenario: The room next door is filled with noise, and you're trying to concentrate.

So What?: Distractions are inevitable. Find a way to focus on what matters and tune out the rest.

Lesson: Noise is temporary, but your focus can be constant. A little mindfulness goes a long way.

CHAPTER 34
The Forgotten Password

Scenario: You forgot your login details—again—and now you're locked out.

So What?: Reset it, and don't beat yourself up. Technology was made to trip us up sometimes.

Lesson: Small hiccups don't define your day. Solutions are just a click away.

CHAPTER 35
Playing Office Chess, Not Checkers

Scenario: In the game of Office life, some people play checkers—making quick, obvious moves, reacting to what's right in front of them. But not you. You're playing chess. You're five moves ahead, strategically planning your next steps, predicting workplace dynamics, and setting yourself up for future success. All the while, your colleagues think you're just casually sipping coffee in meetings, but in reality, you're low-key plotting your next career victory.

So What?: The trick to playing Office chess is subtlety. You're not openly scheming for promotions or world domination (just kidding... kind of). Instead, you're building relationships, observing patterns, and positioning yourself for key opportunities without making it obvious. While others are busy reacting to today's problems, you're already solving tomorrow's. Patience is your greatest asset—wait for the right moment, then make your move.

Lesson: In the workplace, thinking ahead is a superpower. By approaching your career like a chessboard—carefully choosing your actions and anticipating outcomes—you're setting yourself up for long-term success. It's not about making the fastest moves; it's about making the smartest ones. So, keep playing chess while everyone else plays checkers. Just remember: world domination works best when no one suspects it's happening.

CHAPTER 36
The Casual Friday Confusion

Scenario: You thought it was casual Friday, but it wasn't.

So What?: Confidence is everything. If you own it, no one will question it.

Lesson: Dress codes come and go, but your self-assurance is what truly leaves an impression.

CHAPTER 37
The Overbooked Calendar

Scenario: Your calendar is packed, and now you're double-booked for meetings.

So What?: Reschedule, delegate, or send someone in your place. Everyone's busy, and people understand.

Lesson: Time management is about balance. Sometimes it's okay to say no or adjust.

CHAPTER 38
The Undercover Leader

Scenario: You're not the boss, you don't have an oficial leadership title, but somehow, you're the one making things happen. Your team turns to you for answers, you subtly steer meetings in the right direction, and you're basically organizing the chaos without anyone even noticing. You're like Batman, silently swooping in to save the day without needing the spotlight—or a cape.

So What?: Keep embracing your stealthy leadership! Not every hero needs a title to get the job done. As long as the team is moving forward and projects are running smoothly, does it really matter who gets the credit? The key to being an undercover leader is guiding the group with subtle suggestions, nudging people in the right direction, and making decisions that move the team forward—all while remaining humble and low-key. You're the quiet force behind the scenes, and no one needs to know that you're secretly the glue holding it all together.

Lesson: Leadership isn't about titles; it's about influence. Whether you're oficially in charge or just the unoficial go-to person, your impact speaks louder than any formal role. Keep leading from the shadows, Batman—you're exactly what your team needs, even if they don't realize it.

CHAPTER 39
The Forgotten Meeting

Scenario: You completely forgot about a meeting until you got a reminder.

So What?: Apologize and join in. It happens to the best of us. The key is showing up and contributing when you can.

Lesson: Forgetting happens, but being proactive makes the difference.

CHAPTER 40
The Copycat Colleague

Scenario: A colleague keeps copying your ideas or taking credit for your work.

So What?: They can copy your ideas, but they can't copy your creativity. Keep pushing out great work—authenticity always shines through.

Lesson: True talent can't be copied, and recognition will come to those who earn it.

CHAPTER 41
The "No Alcohol" Commitment in a Sea of Happy Hour Enthusiasts

Scenario: You've sworn off alcohol for health or mindfulness, but your team is all about after-work drinks and office parties. While they're clinking glasses, you're the odd one out with your sparkling water.

So What?: Own it! No one really cares what's in your glass, and you'll have just as much fun—minus the hangover. Plus, you'll be the hero who remembers all the funny stories.

Lesson: Going alcohol-free doesn't mean missing out. Enjoy the energy of the group while staying sharp, and silently celebrate when your colleagues drag themselves into the Office the next day.

CHAPTER 42
The Late Arrival

Scenario: You're late to work because of trafic, and it feels like everyone noticed.

So What?: Life happens. You showed up, and that's what counts. Most people are too busy with their own day to notice your late entrance.

Lesson: Punctuality is great, but what really matters is what you do when you're there.

CHAPTER 43
The Overslept Alarm

Scenario: You hit snooze one too many times and woke up late for work.

So What?: We've all been there. Get ready quickly, and make the best of the day.

Lesson: A late start doesn't mean a bad day. You can still finish strong.

CHAPTER 44
The Performance Review Panic

Scenario: You've got a performance review coming up, and you're nervous.

So What?: Reviews are just moments in time. It's your ongoing effort that truly counts.

Lesson: One review doesn't define you. Stay focused on your long-term growth.

CHAPTER 45
The Empathy Jedi

Scenario: A colleague is having a tough day, but they're not saying anything. You sense their struggle with your Jedi-like emotional intelligence.

So What?: Channel your inner Yoda and offer a subtle, "I'm here if you need me" moment. Sometimes just knowing someone cares is the best support.

Lesson: Empathy doesn't need to be loud. Use the force of kindness to help your colleagues, but don't become their emotional Yoda unless they ask for it.

CHAPTER 46
The Emoji Overload

Scenario: You add a smiley to an email, and before you know it, your message is a parade of emojis—thumbs-ups, party poppers, and even a rogue winking face. What was meant to be a professional email now looks like a text to your best friend.

So What?: While emojis add warmth, less is more in the workplace. One or two? Sure. But an emoji explosion? Maybe not the best look for your boss.

Lesson: Emojis are like hot sauce—use sparingly. Keep it professional, and save the fireworks for a fun text!

CHAPTER 47

The "Forgot the Attachment" Fumble

Scenario: You send off a detailed email, only to get the dreaded reply: "Did you mean to attach the file?" Your stomach drops—classic attachment fail.

So What?: Quickly send a light-hearted follow-up with the file attached. We've all been there, and it's not a big deal.

Lesson: Forgetting the attachment is a harmless workplace blunder. Double-check before hitting send next time, and just own it with a smile.

CHAPTER 48
Zoom Background Bluff

Scenario: It's minutes before your virtual meeting, and your room is a disaster. But with a well-angled camera and a strategically placed plant, you create the illusion of a spotless, Pinterest-worthy workspace.

So What?: Keep the camera focused and pray no one asks you to stand. If the clutter stays hidden, you're golden!

Lesson: In remote work, appearances matter—just not as much as we think. Embrace the chaos outside the frame, and let your Zoom background do the magic.

CHAPTER 49
The Mentorship Maze

Scenario: You've heard all the career advice: "Find a mentor, and your path to success will be paved with golden opportunities!" But finding the perfect mentor feels a lot like hunting for a unicorn—rare, magical, and possibly non-existent. Every time you think you've found one, they either vanish into thin air or are so busy, you feel guilty even scheduling a five-minute chat.

So What?: Don't stress! Mentors come in all shapes and sizes, and you don't need to find the *one* mentor who holds all the answers. Instead, build a network of people who can guide you in different areas—maybe one mentor for leadership advice, another for technical skills, and one more for keeping your sanity. The best part? It doesn't have to be a formal arrangement; sometimes the best mentors don't even know they're mentoring you.

Lesson: Finding the perfect mentor might be a wild goose chase, but piecing together wisdom from different people is just as valuable. Treat mentorship like a buffet—take a little from here, a little from there, and build your own path to greatness!

CHAPTER 50
The Guilt Tug-of-War

Scenario: When you're at work, you feel guilty for not being home. When you're at home, you feel guilty for not doing enough at work. It's like a never-ending mental game of tug-of-war, and no matter where you are, it feels like you're letting someone (or yourself) down.

So What?: Let go of the rope! You're not a superhero with the ability to clone yourself (though that would be handy). The truth is, you're doing the best you can, and that's enough. Work will always be there, and so will home—so stop measuring yourself against impossible standards.

Lesson: Perfection doesn't exist. It's easy to feel like you're not giving enough in either space, but the real win is balancing what you can in the moment. Some days work will take priority, and some days home will—trust that you're doing what's necessary, and give yourself permission to relax without guilt.

CHAPTER 51
The "Am I Allowed to Be Proud?" Dilemma

Scenario: You just crushed a major project, your boss is singing your praises, and your inbox is full of high-fives from colleagues. But instead of basking in the glory, you're sitting there thinking, "Do I even deserve this?"

So What?: You're allowed to feel proud! It's time to stop downplaying your accomplishments and give yourself the credit you deserve. Take a moment to reflect on all the hard work, late nights, and problem-solving that got you here. It's okay to be happy about your success—after all, if you don't celebrate it, who will?

Lesson: Being humble is great, but you don't have to shrink your achievements to fit in. Learn to savor your wins, big or small. Whether it's a solo celebration dance in your living room or treating yourself to your favorite coffee, own your success—it's part of what keeps you growing!

CHAPTER 52

The Green-Eyed You Monster

Scenario: Your colleague just got that promotion you had your eye on, or maybe they've been showered with praise for a project while you feel like you're stuck in the background. Suddenly, the green-eyed monster is lurking inside, and it's not a cute look.

So What?: It's normal to feel a twinge of jealousy, but instead of letting it fester, use it as fuel for self-improvement. Take a step back and ask yourself what you can learn from their success. Do they have skills you can develop? Were they more strategic in how they navigated the project? Turn jealousy into curiosity—and then into action.

Lesson: Jealousy is a sneaky little beast, but it's also a sign that you care about your career. The key is to channel it into positive energy. Celebrate your colleague's success and remember—your time will come, too. In the meantime, focus on your own path and keep leveling up.

CHAPTER 53
The Last-Minute Project

Scenario: You're handed a last-minute project that feels impossible to complete in time.

So What?: Break it down into smaller tasks, focus on one thing at a time, and ask for help if needed.

Lesson: Big tasks are just a series of small ones. Tackle them one step at a time.

CHAPTER 54
The Critical Email

Scenario: You open your inbox to a critical email from your boss about a mistake you didn't even know you made. It feels harsh and unfair.

So What?: Everyone makes mistakes—even bosses. Instead of stewing over it, you fix it, respond politely, and move on. No one remembers those tiny errors in the long run, but they do remember how you handle yourself in the aftermath.

Lesson: Mistakes happen, but they're not permanent marks on who you are. Bounce back, and let your actions do the talking.

CHAPTER 55
The Budget Cuts

Scenario: Your project's budget got cut unexpectedly, making it harder to complete.

So What?: Constraints fuel creativity. Find smarter ways to achieve your goals within the new budget.

Lesson: Great work isn't about big budgets, it's about resourcefulness.

CHAPTER 56
The Out-of-Touch Boss

Scenario: Your boss seems disconnected from the team and unaware of what's happening.

So What?: Keep doing your job well, and communicate regularly to ensure your boss stays in the loop.

Lesson: A proactive approach to communication helps bridge the gap between you and your boss.

CHAPTER 57
The Networking Nightmare

Scenario: You attended a networking event but didn't make any meaningful connections.

So What?: Networking is a long game. Each event is a stepping stone, so don't stress about one-off misses.

Lesson: Building relationships takes time. Every interaction is practice.

CHAPTER 58
The Presentation Interruptions

Scenario: You're constantly interrupted during your presentation, derailing your flow.

So What?: Answer the questions, then guide the conversation back to your main points. Flexibility is key.

Lesson: Presentations aren't just about talking—they're about engaging. Embrace the dialogue.

CHAPTER 59
The Forgotten File

Scenario: You left an important file at home, and now you're scrambling.

So What?: There's always a workaround—go digital, borrow from a colleague, or reschedule.

Lesson: Quick thinking saves the day. Adapt and find a solution.

CHAPTER 60
The Conference Call Fail

Scenario: You forgot to mute your mic during a conference call, and everyone heard your side conversations.

So What?: Apologize, mute, and move on. People have done worse.

Lesson: Mistakes happen—how you recover is what matters.

CHAPTER 61
The Client Ghosting

Scenario: A client stopped replying to your messages, leaving you in limbo.

So What?: People get busy. Follow up politely, but don't let it stress you out.

Lesson: Clients come and go, but your professionalism stays constant.

CHAPTER 62
The Working Weekend

Scenario: You have to work over the weekend, and it feels unfair.

So What?: Sometimes work requires sacrifice. Get through it, then reward yourself with something fun.

Lesson: Balance comes in waves. When you have to work hard, make sure to rest just as hard.

CHAPTER 63
The Over Enthusiastic Team Member

Scenario: A team member is over-the-top excited and dominating every conversation.

So What?: Enthusiasm is contagious. Let them shine, and contribute when it's your time.

Lesson: Every team has different energies. Your moment to shine will come.

CHAPTER 64
The Silent Treatment

Scenario: You share an idea, and the room goes quiet.

So What?: Silence doesn't mean rejection. Sometimes people need time to digest your idea.

Lesson: Don't mistake silence for disinterest. Give it time to sink in.

CHAPTER 65
The Introvert's Survival Challenge

Scenario: It's team-building day—your worst nightmare. A full day of icebreakers, group activities, and trust falls, and all you want to do is hide in the bathroom with your headphones.

So What?: Take a deep breath and remind yourself: you've survived this before, and you'll survive it again. Find your moments of solitude where you can, be the person who takes notes in group discussions (so you can avoid talking), and remember that it's okay to sit out the karaoke portion.

Lesson: Being an introvert in a world full of extroverted activities is like running a marathon in flip-flops. You can still cross the finish line, but it's going to take some strategy. Know your limits, embrace your quiet strengths, and find ways to recharge in the middle of the chaos.

CHAPTER 66

The Salary Expectation vs. Reality Show

Scenario: You sit down for your annual review, hoping for that glorious moment where your boss says, "We're giving you a 50% raise!" Instead, you hear, "We're offering a 3% cost-of-living adjustment... isn't that exciting?"

So What?: Sure, it's not the raise you imagined while daydreaming at your desk, but don't let it deflate your enthusiasm. Keep the conversation open, set clear goals for your next review, and maybe start practicing your happy face for that next 3%.

Lesson: Salary discussions can be awkward, but they're just one part of the bigger picture. You might not walk away with a fortune, but you can walk away with a plan—and that's worth a lot more than a polite "thank you" for 3%.

CHAPTER 67
The Work-Life Balance Sweet Spot

Scenario: You've found that magical place where work and life actually coexist in harmony. You're getting your tasks done, feeling fulfilled at work, and still managing to squeeze in time for hobbies, family, and maybe even a yoga class or two.

So What?: Keep nurturing that balance! It's easy to get pulled into overwork or, on the flip side, let work slide when life gets busy. But you've cracked the code by setting boundaries and sticking to them. Share your tips with colleagues who might be struggling—they'll appreciate the support.

Lesson: True work-life balance is about finding a rhythm that works for you and your responsibilities. It's not about perfection—it's about knowing when to push and when to pull back. When you master that, everything flows more smoothly.

CHAPTER 68
The Favoritism Fiasco

Scenario: It's clear as day—your boss has a favorite, and it's not you. They get the best projects, all the praise, and, let's face it, way too many coffee breaks with the higher-ups.

So What?: Don't waste your energy playing the favoritism game. Focus on excelling in your own lane, building relationships with others, and showing your value through results, not Office politics.

Lesson: Favoritism happens, but it doesn't define your worth. Let your work and professionalism shine, and trust that consistent effort will get noticed in the long run—even if you're not the boss's pet.

CHAPTER 69
The Colleague Competition Showdown

Scenario: Your colleagues are turning every meeting into a showdown, constantly trying to one-up you, and it's getting really annoying.

So What?: Take a deep breath and remember: this isn't *Survivor*, and you don't need to vote anyone off the island. Focus on doing your best work, and let them waste their energy on unnecessary competition.

Lesson: When colleagues are openly competing with you, don't get sucked into the drama. Be the calm in the storm, and let your work speak louder than their antics. In the end, substance always beats showmanship.

CHAPTER 70
The Knowledge Sponge 2.0

Scenario: Another workplace trend is taking over, and it's your chance to absorb and evolve.

So What?: Become the go-to person on this new tool, system, or trend by diving deep and mastering it quickly.

Lesson: When you're the knowledge sponge of the team, you never stop growing. Keep soaking it all up, and soon everyone will turn to you for answers.

CHAPTER 71
The Integrity Ninja

Scenario: There's pressure to take a shortcut, but your internal Integrity Ninja tells you otherwise.

So What?: Stick to your ethical guns. Even if it's the harder path now, you know it's the right one. Your stealthy integrity will pay off.

Lesson: Integrity is a quiet, stealthy superpower. You don't need to shout about it—just live by it.

CHAPTER 72
The Feedback Dance-Off

Scenario: You've been asked to give constructive feedback, but you know it's a tricky conversation.

So What?: Time to put on your dancing shoes and deliver that feedback with a careful two-step of kindness and honesty.

Lesson: Feedback is an art, not a battle. If you can master the delicate dance, everyone walks away feeling better.

CHAPTER 73

The Avengers Assemble Moment

Scenario: Your team is facing a huge challenge, and everyone has different strengths. It's time to assemble your workplace Avengers.

So What?: Call upon your team's superpowers and lead them to victory, making sure everyone uses their unique talents to crush the project.

Lesson: Great teamwork is about knowing when to call in the specialists. When the team unites like superheroes, there's no stopping you.

CHAPTER 74
The MacGyver Moment

Scenario: You're given an impossible task with zero resources, but you've watched enough *MacGyver* to know there's a solution in there somewhere.

So What?: Don't panic! Embrace the challenge, and approach it with a fresh perspective. Sometimes, all you need is some quick thinking, a little innovation, and a willingness to improvise—because real creativity shines under pressure.

Lesson: With creativity and resourcefulness, you can solve almost anything. Who needs fancy tools when your best asset is your ingenuity?

CHAPTER 75
The Exit Interview

Scenario: A colleague is leaving, and you're feeling the loss during their exit interview.

So What?: Change is part of life. Wish them well and focus on building new connections.

Lesson: People come and go, but the relationships you build make lasting impacts.

CHAPTER 76
The Overbooked Travel Schedule

Scenario: Your work travel schedule is packed, and you're feeling drained.

So What?: Travel is tough, but it's an opportunity to see new places and make new connections.

Lesson: Take it one trip at a time, and remember that rest is key.

CHAPTER 77
The Copy Machine Conundrum

Scenario: You're struggling with the Office copier, and nothing seems to work.

So What?: It's just a machine. Take a deep breath, ask for help, or switch to a digital solution.

Lesson: Technology may fail, but your adaptability never does.

CHAPTER 78
The Morning Coffee Spill

Scenario: You spill coffee on yourself right before a big meeting.

So What?: It's a small hiccup. Focus on the meeting, not the stain.

Lesson: Looks fade, but your professionalism shines.

CHAPTER 79
The Forgetful Colleague

Scenario: A colleague forgets an important detail that causes a setback for the project.

So What?: Mistakes happen. Help them out, and keep things moving forward.

Lesson: Teamwork is about lifting each other up when someone slips.

CHAPTER 80
The Office Fridge Fiasco

Scenario: Someone keeps taking your lunch from the Office fridge.

So What?: It's annoying, but it's not worth losing your cool over. Label your food or bring something different.

Lesson: Some battles aren't worth fighting—focus on what matters.

CHAPTER 81
The Micromanaging Boss

Scenario: Your boss is micromanaging every little detail, and it's frustrating.

So What?: Communicate your progress clearly to build trust, and show that you can handle things independently.

Lesson: Trust is earned through consistent effort and clear communication.

CHAPTER 82
The Elevator Pitch Gone Wrong

Scenario: You gave a less-than-perfect elevator pitch to a senior leader.

So What?: Not every moment is a win. There will be more opportunities to shine.

Lesson: One misstep doesn't define your whole career. Keep refining your pitch.

CHAPTER 83
The Broken Chair Incident

Scenario: You sat on a chair, and it broke in the middle of a meeting.

So What?: Laugh it off and keep going. A little physical mishap doesn't change your contribution to the meeting.

Lesson: Laughter is the best recovery from awkward moments.

CHAPTER 84
The Surprise Office Visit

Scenario: A client or senior leader shows up at the Office unexpectedly, and you're unprepared.

So What?: You're adaptable. Show them around, and keep things casual.

Lesson: A little spontaneity keeps things interesting. Be ready to roll with surprises.

CHAPTER 85
The Delayed Feedback

Scenario: You're waiting on feedback for an important project, and it's delayed.

So What?: Use the time to refine or reflect. Feedback will come, and you'll be ready to improve.

Lesson: Patience pays off. Sometimes waiting is part of the process.

CHAPTER 86
The Conference Room Double-Booking

Scenario: Your meeting room got double-booked, and now there's a scramble for space.

So What?: Find an alternative space, or suggest a virtual meeting. Problem solved.

Lesson: Flexibility in the workplace helps you pivot quickly when plans change.

CHAPTER 87
The Chatty Co-Worker

Scenario: Your coworker won't stop talking when you're trying to focus.

So What?: Politely excuse yourself or redirect the conversation. You're in control of your time.

Lesson: Boundaries can be set with kindness. You don't have to engage in every conversation.

CHAPTER 88

The Misunderstood comment

Scenario: You made a comment, and it wasn't taken the way you intended.

So What?: Clarify your intention if needed, and move on. Not every comment will land.

Lesson: Don't sweat it when a comment doesn't hit the mark.

CHAPTER 89
The Endless Conference Call

Scenario: The conference call that should have ended 20 minutes ago just keeps going.

So What?: Hang in there. Stay engaged, and mentally prep your escape plan when it's done.

Lesson: Not all meetings are eficient, but your patience is valuable.

CHAPTER 90
The Unreturned Call

Scenario: You've been waiting for a return call from an important contact, and it's not coming.

So What?: Give them some time. People are busy, and they'll get back to you when they can.

Lesson: Patience is part of professional communication.

CHAPTER 91
The No-Show Interviewee

Scenario: You've prepped for an interview, but the candidate never shows up.

So What?: People flake sometimes. Reschedule or move on to the next.

Lesson: Missed appointments happen, but they're not worth stressing over.

CHAPTER 92
The Overlapping Deadlines

Scenario: You have two major deadlines on the same day, and you're overwhelmed.

So What?: Prioritize, delegate, and communicate with your team if extensions are needed.

Lesson: Deadlines are important, but communication is key to managing them well.

CHAPTER 93
The Confusing Office Jargon

Scenario: You're in a meeting, and people are throwing around jargon you don't understand.

So What?: Ask for clarification or do a quick search later. No one knows everything.

Lesson: You don't have to know it all, but you can always learn.

CHAPTER 94
The Silent Office Party

Scenario: The Office party is awkwardly silent, and no one's breaking the ice.

So What?: Be the one to start the conversation or suggest a fun activity.

Lesson: Social dynamics are part of work life, but they don't have to be intimidating.

CHAPTER 95
The Overly Complicated Password Policy

Scenario: It's time to change your password—again—and the system requires uppercase letters, lowercase letters, numbers, symbols, hieroglyphics, and possibly a blood oath. Oh, and you can't reuse any of your last 20 passwords.

So What?: It's a pain, but it's a necessary evil in the world of digital security. Just remember, no one ever gets the password right on the first try.

Lesson: Password policies are like a secret challenge designed to test your patience. But hey, at least you're probably better protected than Fort Knox now.

CHAPTER 96
The Meeting That Could Have Been an Email

Scenario: You spent an hour in a meeting that could have been handled in a short email.

So What?: Take it in stride. At least you had face-to-face time. Next time, suggest an email instead.

Lesson: Meetings aren't always eficient, but they're still a part of the work culture.

CHAPTER 97
The Tech Glitch Disaster

Scenario: Your computer crashes right before an important deadline, and you lose your work.

So What?: Restart, recover what you can, and learn from it. Tech failures are inevitable, but your persistence is key.

Lesson: Always backup your files.. And when things go wrong, stay calm. Be honest, ask to extend the deadline, apologize and do it again.

CHAPTER 98
The Office Rivalry

Scenario: There's tension between you and a colleague, and it's becoming a rivalry.

So What?: Focus on your own work. Rivals can be motivating, but don't let them consume you.

Lesson: Competition is healthy, but personal growth is your true goal.

CHAPTER 99
The Oversharing Colleague

Scenario: A colleague keeps oversharing personal details, and it's getting awkward.

So What?: Redirect the conversation back to work or politely disengage when needed.

Lesson: Boundaries are essential for maintaining professionalism, even with chatty colleagues.

CHAPTER 100
The "What Do You Think About Them?" Colleague

Scenario: You're casually chatting in the break room when your colleague leans in and asks, "So, what do you think about [insert coworker's name here]?" You already know where this is going. This colleague is always on a secret mission to gather intel on everyone in the Office—whether it's opinions about the boss, the new hire, or even the lunch choices of the guy from accounting. It's like they're running an unofficial workplace gossip survey.

So What?: Time to tread carefully! Don't get sucked into the trap of critiquing others or spilling your thoughts. Instead, go for the neutral "Oh, they seem nice!" and watch the conversation fade into harmless territory. Bonus points if you turn the question back on them: "What do *you* think?"—you'll see them scramble!

Lesson: When your colleague is on a "what do you think about them" mission, stay neutral and dodge the gossip trap. In the Office, some things are better left unsaid—especially when they're about someone else.

CHAPTER 101
The Group Project Dilemma

Scenario: You're in a group project, and one person isn't pulling their weight.

So What?: Address it directly or take on what you can. Every group has its slackers.

Lesson: Collaboration isn't always perfect, but clear communication can help.

CHAPTER 102
The Mystery Meeting Invitation

Scenario: You're added to a meeting invite and have no idea why you're there. The subject is vague, the participants are unfamiliar, and as the conversation unfolds, it becomes clear that you have absolutely nothing to contribute. You sit there, nodding thoughtfully, praying no one asks for your opinion.

So What?: Relax! Every meeting has a few extras who aren't quite sure why they're there. Just focus on looking engaged, sprinkle in the occasional "good point," and remember: if you're not speaking, you're learning!

Lesson: Not every meeting needs your expertise—sometimes you're just there for moral support or to nod wisely. And hey, at least it's not your project that's in chaos!

CHAPTER 103
The Messy Whiteboard

Scenario: The whiteboard in the meeting room is a chaotic mess of scribbles and unfinished ideas from another team.

So What?: A little clutter never stopped a great idea. Wipe it clean, and let your brilliance take center stage.

Lesson: A fresh start is only a clean slate away—literally!

CHAPTER 104

The Unexpected Office Fire Drill

Scenario: You're in the middle of an important task when the fire alarm goes off, and you're forced to evacuate the building.

So What?: Safety first! A little fresh air never hurt anyone, and you'll come back with a clearer head. Bonus: It's an unplanned break.

Lesson: Sometimes, unexpected breaks give you just the right pause to refresh.

CHAPTER 105
The Broken Printer

Scenario: You urgently need to print something, but the Office printer is on the fritz—again.

So What?: Printers have a mind of their own. There's always another printer or a digital workaround. You've got this covered, no matter what the tech throws at you.

Lesson: Tech failure is temporary, but your adaptability is endless.

CHAPTER 106
The Disastrous First Day

Scenario: You're new to the of ice, and your first day is a complete mess—wrong directions, missed introductions, and a confusing schedule.

So What?: Everyone's had a rough first day. What matters is how you pick yourself up and get back in the game. You'll be running the show in no time.

Lesson: First impressions aren't everything. Keep going, and soon you'll settle in.

CHAPTER 107
The Team Outing Gone Wrong

Scenario: Your team planned a fun outing, but everything that could go wrong does—bad weather, canceled reservations, and a lost colleague.

So What?: It's all part of the adventure. Laugh it off, make the most of it, and remember, the point was to have fun, not perfection.

Lesson: Team spirit isn't built on perfect plans—it's built on shared experiences, even the messy ones.

CHAPTER 108
The Unreliable Wi-Fi

Scenario: You're in the middle of a critical video call when the Wi-Fi drops, leaving you frozen on screen.

So What?: Technical glitches are par for the course. Take a moment to reset, reconnect, and carry on like a pro. Bonus: Everyone's been there, and no one holds it against you.

Lesson: Tech issues are a part of modern work life. Patience and a quick reset are your best tools.

CHAPTER 109
The Last-Minute Client Request

Scenario: A client sends a big, last-minute request right before you're about to call it a day.

So What?: It's the nature of the job. You've handled curveballs before, and you'll handle this one too. A quick adjustment, and you're back in control.

Lesson: Flexibility and quick thinking keep you on top of your game, even when clients throw last-minute surprises.

CHAPTER 110
The Holiday Work Rush

Scenario: The holidays are just around the corner, and your workload has doubled.

So What?: It happens every year, but you always get through it. Prioritize, delegate where possible, and remember—you've got holiday cheer waiting at the end of the tunnel!

Lesson: Holiday work crunches come and go. Focus on getting through it so you can enjoy the break that follows.

CHAPTER 111
The Unrealistic Deadline

Scenario: Your boss gives you a deadline that's impossible to meet without working around the clock.

So What?: Deadlines are flexible, and so are you. Manage expectations, communicate early, and get help if needed. You're not a superhero (though you come pretty close).

Lesson: Unrealistic demands call for clear communication. It's better to set expectations than to burn out.

CHAPTER 112
The Inconsistent Policies

Scenario: Office policies seem to change every week, and no one knows what the real rules are.

So What?: Flexibility is your superpower. Policies will come and go, but your adaptability will keep you grounded.

Lesson: Focus on what you can control. Changes happen, but your ability to adapt is what matters.

CHAPTER 113
The Missed Opportunity

Scenario: You let a great opportunity pass you by, and now you're kicking yourself.

So What?: Life is full of opportunities, and you'll catch the next one. Dwelling on the past won't change it, but learning from it will get you ready for the future.

Lesson: Missed opportunities aren't final. Learn, grow, and get ready for the next big chance.

CHAPTER 114
The Never-Ending To-Do List

Scenario: Your to-do list feels like a Hydra—every time you check one thing off, two more tasks appear. It's overwhelming.

So What?: There will always be work, and no one expects you to do it all at once. Take it one task at a time, and remember, you're only human. Prioritize what matters, and the rest will wait.

Lesson: Work doesn't control you. You control how you approach it. Take a breath, tackle what you can, and the world won't end if something waits until tomorrow.

CHAPTER 115
The Lost Key Card

Scenario: You misplaced your Office key card and can't get into the building.

So What?: These things happen! Ask security for help, and enjoy a mini-break while you wait.

Lesson: Lost key cards are temporary, but your resourcefulness is permanent.

CHAPTER 116

The Office Temperature Battle

Scenario: Half the Office is freezing while the other half is roasting, and no one can agree on the temperature.

So What?: Layers are your best friend. Find a comfy balance, or keep a cozy sweater nearby.

Lesson: You can't control the thermostat, but you can control how you handle the heat (or cold).

CHAPTER 117
The Loud Typist

Scenario: A colleague types so loudly it sounds like they're pounding on the keyboard.

So What?: It's just background noise. Plug in some headphones or tune it out—you're bigger than the sound.

Lesson: Some Office noise is inevitable. Find your focus despite the distraction.

CHAPTER 118
The Printer Paper Jam

Scenario: You're in a rush, and the printer jams right when you need to print something important.

So What?: Printers are unpredictable. Fix the jam or ask for help, but don't let it throw off your day.

Lesson: Small inconveniences shouldn't derail your focus. You're flexible enough to handle them.

CHAPTER 119
The Unread Newsletter

Scenario: You spent time writing a company newsletter, and no one seems to be reading it.

So What?: You've done your part, and the info is out there. Keep improving your content and let people catch up when they can.

Lesson: Sometimes people miss things, but the effort you put in is still valuable.

CHAPTER 120

The Forgotten Phone Charger

Scenario: You forgot your phone charger, and your battery is at 5%.

So What?: You'll survive. Find a charging station or borrow one from a coworker, and unplug for a bit in the meantime.

Lesson: Small missteps are no big deal. You can always find a way to recharge.

CHAPTER 121
The Inbox Full of Spam

Scenario: Your inbox is clogged with junk mail, making it hard to find important emails.

So What?: Clean it out and stay on top of it. A little digital housekeeping will make your life easier.

Lesson: Digital clutter is easy to fix. Regular maintenance is your key to inbox sanity.

CHAPTER 122
The Misspelled Name

Scenario: You accidentally misspelled someone's name in an important email.

So What?: A quick apology will fix it. We've all made typos, and most people don't mind.

Lesson: Mistakes happen, but a polite correction shows professionalism.

CHAPTER 123
The Overly Complex Spreadsheet

Scenario: You open a spreadsheet, and it's a labyrinth of confusing formulas and data.

So What?: Take a deep breath, start simple, and figure it out one step at a time.

Lesson: Big challenges are solved with small, focused actions.

CHAPTER 124
The Office Microwave Meltdown

Scenario: Someone overheats their lunch in the Office microwave, and now the break room smells like burned popcorn.

So What?: It's annoying, but the smell will pass. Open a window, have a laugh, and move on.

Lesson: Tiny inconveniences don't have to ruin your day. Keep perspective.

CHAPTER 125
The Mr./Miss Know-It-All Showdown

Scenario: You're in a meeting, and *that* colleague strikes again—Mr./Miss Know-It-All. No matter the topic, they have all the answers, all the solutions, and somehow, even though the conversation was about Office supplies, they're suddenly an expert on international logistics and quantum physics. You nod politely while secretly wondering if they've ever uttered the phrase, "I don't know." Spoiler: they haven't.

So What?: The trick to surviving a Know-It-All? Let them have their moment in the sun. Nod, smile, and let them explain the obvious with the enthusiasm of someone who's just discovered gravity. Then, drop in your own knowledge casually, like a stealthy ninja. They may never stop being a Know-It-All, but you can outsmart them by being quietly confident—and not needing to know everything.

Lesson: Mr./Miss Know-It-All may think they have all the answers, but that doesn't mean you have to compete. Let them flex their trivia muscles while you stay calm, cool, and knowledgeable in your own right. Sometimes, the best move is knowing when *not* to say anything.

CHAPTER 126
The Team "Too Many Cooks" Moment

Scenario: Everyone on the team has an opinion, but no one's taking ownership of the project.

So What?: Step up and take the lead, or help organize the chaos. Teams need direction, and sometimes that means stepping out of the crowd.

Lesson: Leadership doesn't require a title. Sometimes, taking initiative is all it takes.

CHAPTER 127

The Micro-Aggression Moment

Scenario: A subtle comment in a meeting makes you or a colleague feel uncomfortable, but no one addresses it.

So What?: Don't let it slide. Gently but assertively call it out and create space for a more respectful conversation.

Lesson: Addressing micro-aggressions is important for creating a healthier, more inclusive workplace. Speak up with kindness, but stand firm.

CHAPTER 128
The Boss Who's All Talk, No Action

Scenario: Your boss keeps promising big changes, but nothing ever seems to happen.

So What?: Don't rely on promises. Focus on what you can control, and keep doing your job well. Change will come eventually.

Lesson: Actions speak louder than words. Keep delivering results, and opportunities will follow.

CHAPTER 129
The Technology Takeover

Scenario: Your company has introduced a new software system, and everyone's struggling to adapt.

So What?: Every new tool comes with a learning curve. Embrace the challenge, and soon you'll be the Office expert.

Lesson: Technology is a tool, not a hurdle. Master it, and you'll streamline your work life.

CHAPTER 130
The Team That Missed the Mark

Scenario: Your team just finished a project, but it didn't turn out the way you planned.

So What?: Learn from it, discuss what went wrong, and move on to the next challenge with new insights.

Lesson: Failure is part of growth. Teams that learn from mistakes are the ones that succeed in the long run.

CHAPTER 131
The Silent Power Struggle

Scenario: You sense there's a silent power struggle happening in your team, but no one is openly discussing it.

So What?: Address the elephant in the room. Bring everyone together, get the issues out in the open, and work toward collaboration.

Lesson: Transparency clears the air, and teamwork thrives when hidden agendas are brought into the light.

CHAPTER 132
The "I Forgot the Time Zone" Mix-Up

Scenario: You forgot about time zones and scheduled a meeting at the wrong time for your international colleagues.

So What?: Reschedule, apologize, and be more mindful next time. Time zones are tricky, and people understand.

Lesson: Global teams require extra attention to detail. Time zone mishaps are just learning opportunities.

CHAPTER 133
The Boss Who Changes Their Mind

Scenario: You're halfway through a project, and your boss decides they want to go in a completely different direction.

So What?: Flexibility is your superpower. Adapt, adjust, and remind yourself that every change is just another way to improve.

Lesson: Leadership can be unpredictable, but your adaptability makes you indispensable.

CHAPTER 134
The "Wrong Zoom Room" Fiasco

Scenario: You joined the wrong Zoom meeting and sat awkwardly in silence before realizing it.

So What?: It happens! Excuse yourself politely, and join the right room. Everyone's been there.

Lesson: Mistakes are human. Laugh it off and move forward.

CHAPTER 135
The Subordinate with Big Ideas

Scenario: One of your team members always has big, ambitious ideas, but they rarely follow through.

So What?: Help guide them into realistic actions. Big ideas are great, but execution is where the magic happens.

Lesson: Vision needs structure. Great leadership helps turn dreams into reality.

CHAPTER 136
The Office Gossip Gauntlet

Scenario: People are gossiping, and it's making the rounds in the Office.

So What?: Stay above the fray. Focus on your work and avoid engaging in the rumor mill. Your reputation will thank you later.

Lesson: Silence is powerful. Sometimes the best response to gossip is no response at all.

CHAPTER 137
The Subtle Sabotage

Scenario: You suspect someone on your team is subtly undermining your efforts, but it's hard to prove.

So What?: Rise above it. Focus on your work, and let your results speak for themselves. Eventually, their behavior will come to light.

Lesson: Integrity outlasts sabotage. Stay focused on doing your best work, and let others dig their own holes.

CHAPTER 138

The "We Don't Know What We're Doing" Project

Scenario: Your team is given a project, but no one has a clue how to tackle it.

So What?: Break it down into smaller tasks, research what you need to, and start somewhere—progress will follow.

Lesson: You don't have to know everything upfront. Just take the first step, and the rest will follow.

CHAPTER 139
The Boss Who Can't Let Go

Scenario: Your boss is having trouble delegating and insists on doing everything themselves.

So What?: Offer to take small tasks off their plate, and show them that delegation can make the whole team stronger.

Lesson: Great teams thrive on trust. Help your boss see that they don't have to carry the load alone.

CHAPTER 140
The Values Clash

Scenario: You're working on a project that conflicts with your personal values.

So What?: Speak up and have an honest conversation about your concerns. You may find solutions that align better with your values.

Lesson: Integrity is priceless. Don't compromise your values for short-term gains.

CHAPTER 141
The "Is This Really My Job?" Moment

Scenario: You find yourself doing a random task that has nothing to do with your actual job description.

So What?: Sometimes you just have to roll with it. Every odd job teaches you something—even if it's just patience.

Lesson: No task is too small, and every random moment can add to your skill set, even if it's not what you signed up for.

CHAPTER 142
The Last-Minute Presentation Hero

Scenario: You get asked to give a presentation at the last minute, and you haven't prepared anything.

So What?: Improvise! Your experience and confidence will carry you through. Just make sure to smile and keep things simple.

Lesson: Sometimes the best presentations are the ones you didn't have time to overthink.

CHAPTER 143
The "Forgot My Pants" Dream

Scenario: You have a dream that you showed up to work without pants.

So What?: Relax! It's just a dream. Everyone has those weird work nightmares, but they don't define reality.

Lesson: Stress dreams are just your brain's way of letting off steam. Laugh at them and move on!

CHAPTER 144

The Too Many Buzzwords Meeting

Scenario: Your meeting turns into a game of corporate buzzword bingo—synergy, pivot, value-add, and you're drowning in jargon.

So What?: Smile, nod, and mentally check off those buzzwords. You know what's really important: cutting through the fluff.

Lesson: Buzzwords don't do the work—people do. Keep things simple, and focus on the real tasks.

CHAPTER 145
The All-Day Meeting Marathon

Scenario: Your day is jam-packed with back-to-back meetings, and you feel like you're drowning.

So What?: Embrace the meeting marathon with snacks, coffee, and a positive attitude. Tomorrow is a fresh start!

Lesson: You can survive anything with good snacks, a sense of humor, and some solid note-taking.

CHAPTER 146

The "What Was My Point Again?"

Scenario: You're mid-sentence in a meeting, and you completely forget what you were talking about.

So What?: It happens to everyone! Smile, pause, and ask for a moment to regroup. People will appreciate your honesty.

Lesson: Confidence is key. Even when you forget your point, staying calm keeps you in control.

CHAPTER 147

The Never-Ending Spreadsheet

Scenario: You're working on a spreadsheet, and every time you think you're done, more data appears.

So What?: Spreadsheets are like a black hole—they suck you in. Embrace the zen of endless data, and remember there's always Ctrl+Z.

Lesson: Perfection is overrated. Done is better than perfect, and spreadsheets will never truly be finished!

CHAPTER 148
The Epic IT Fail

Scenario: Your computer crashes in the middle of a big project, and you didn't save.

So What?: It's the ultimate facepalm moment, but you'll survive. Rebuild, recover, and take it as a lesson to always hit save.

Lesson: Technology fails, but resilience doesn't. You can always recover, and the second version is often better.

CHAPTER 149

The Email Typos You Missed

Scenario: You hit "send" on an email, only to realize afterward it's riddled with typos.

So What?: Perfection is a myth. Most people won't even notice—or they've done the same thing themselves!

Lesson: It's not the typos that matter—it's the follow-up. Keep the conversation going, and no one will remember the mistakes.

CHAPTER 150
The "Can't Stop Laughing" Meeting

Scenario: Something ridiculous happens in a meeting, and now you and a colleague can't stop giggling.

So What?: Laughter is contagious and healthy! As long as it's harmless, enjoy the light moment, then refocus when you're ready.

Lesson: Humor can break tension and build bonds. Sometimes a shared laugh is exactly what your team needs.

CHAPTER 151
The End-of-Day Energy Crash

Scenario: It's 3 p.m., and your energy hits rock bottom just as your to-do list peaks.

So What?: Grab a coffee, take a quick walk, or power through—whatever works for you. Energy ebbs and flows; it's normal.

Lesson: Productivity isn't linear. Don't beat yourself up over a slump—just adjust and carry on.

CHAPTER 152
The "Do It My Way" Colleague

Scenario: You've got a colleague who *always* insists that everyone should do things *exactly* their way—from how to arrange files to the perfect way to organize a team lunch. No matter the task, they're ready with an unsolicited opinion, eager to mold you into their mini-clone.

So What?: Let them talk, nod along, and then do it your way (the right way, of course!). You're not here to be anyone's puppet. Sometimes the best way to handle these "my way or the highway" types is to politely agree and then casually go rogue. Let's face it, variety is the spice of life!

Lesson: Everyone has their quirks, and sometimes it's about finding a middle ground between humoring their insistence and staying true to your style. Your uniqueness is what makes you valuable at work, not your ability to follow someone else's instructions to a tee.

CHAPTER 153

The Return from Vacation Overload

Scenario: You come back from vacation to an inbox flooded with unread emails.

So What?: Prioritize, tackle what's urgent, and let go of the rest. It's a natural part of the post-vacation catch-up game.

Lesson: You don't have to do everything at once. Focus on what's important, and ease back into the swing of things.

CHAPTER 154
The Never-Ending Notifications

Scenario: Your phone, email, and chat apps are constantly pinging with notifications, and you can't keep up.

So What?: Turn off the noise! You're in control of your notifications, not the other way around.

Lesson: Digital balance is key to sanity. Set boundaries and unplug when needed.

CHAPTER 155
The Rogue Autocorrect

Scenario: Autocorrect changes an innocent word in your email to something hilarious or awkward.

So What?: It's embarrassing, but it happens to everyone. Send a quick correction, and enjoy the laugh.

Lesson: Autocorrect is a trickster, but a quick follow-up keeps you professional and human.

CHAPTER 156
The Boss's Unclear Instructions

Scenario: Your boss gives you a vague assignment, and you're not sure what they're asking for.

So What?: Ask for clarification! No one expects mind reading. It's better to ask now than to redo it later.

Lesson: Clarity saves time and frustration. Don't be afraid to ask questions early.

CHAPTER 157
The "I Forgot My Password Again" Day

Scenario: You forgot your password for the hundredth time, and now you're locked out of your system.

So What?: Reset it, write it down this time, and carry on. Passwords are just a hurdle, not a roadblock.

Lesson: Forgetfulness is human. Be patient with yourself, and find tools to make your life easier.

CHAPTER 158
The Personal Errand at Work

Scenario: You had to run a personal errand during work hours, and now you feel guilty.

So What?: Life happens! Just make up the time, and don't stress over the little things.

Lesson: Work-life balance is about give and take. Sometimes personal errands sneak into work, and that's okay.

CHAPTER 159
The Misinterpreted Email Tone

Scenario: You sent a simple email, but the recipient misinterpreted your tone as cold or harsh.

So What?: Clarify your message with a follow-up call or email, and use emojis or softer language next time.

Lesson: Email tone is tricky—better to over-communicate than to leave things unclear.

CHAPTER 160
The Printer Paper Panic

Scenario: You're in the middle of a huge print job, and halfway through, the printer screams for more paper. You scramble to find some, only to realize it's located in a mysterious closet no one can access without a sacred key (which is, of course, missing).

So What?: Embrace the thrill of the paper chase! Office paper runs are like a scavenger hunt, and when you finally find that ream, it's victory.

Lesson: Office supplies are elusive treasures, but persistence pays off. Just make sure you're not the one who left the printer empty for the next person.

CHAPTER 161
The Office Party Mishap

Scenario: At the Office holiday party, you accidentally spill your drink on your boss.

So What?: Apologize quickly, offer a napkin, and laugh it off. These things happen, and a little humor goes a long way.

Lesson: Mistakes at social events can be turned into fun memories. Own it with grace, and people will forget about it faster than you think.

CHAPTER 162
The Working Lunch Confusion

Scenario: You thought it was a casual lunch with colleagues, but it turns into an intense work meeting.

So What?: Go with the flow. It's not the relaxing break you expected, but it's a chance to show your adaptability.

Lesson: Work can sneak into unexpected places—always be ready to pivot!

CHAPTER 163
The Imposter Syndrome Attack

Scenario: You've just achieved something big, but you feel like a fraud who doesn't deserve it.

So What?: Everyone feels imposter syndrome at some point. Remind yourself of your hard work and accomplishments—you're where you are because you earned it.

Lesson: Self-doubt is normal, but don't let it steal your joy. You've earned your success!

CHAPTER 164
The Rare Boss Compliment

Scenario: You're working away, minding your own business, when out of nowhere, your boss—who is notorious for being as stingy with compliments as a squirrel hoarding acorns—drops a rare gem: "Good job." For a second, you think you misheard. Was that an actual compliment? From *them*? You look around to see if anyone else witnessed this historic event.

So What?: Cherish it. Frame it. Write it down for posterity. It may never happen again. But don't let it go to your head! That compliment is like spotting a unicorn—you've seen it once, and now it'll vanish back into the forest of stoic silence. The key is to nod professionally, thank them, and quietly revel in the miracle that just occurred.

Lesson: When the boss, known for guarding compliments like a dragon guards treasure, actually gives you one, take it as a sign that you've done something truly extraordinary. Just don't hold your breath waiting for the next one. Who knows? You might get another...in about five years.

CHAPTER 165

The Unexpected Work Travel

Scenario: You're suddenly asked to travel for work with little notice, and it throws your personal plans off balance.

So What?: Embrace the adventure! While it's not ideal timing, business trips offer new experiences and opportunities.

Lesson: Flexibility is your superpower. Life rarely goes according to plan, but new opportunities are often hidden in the chaos.

CHAPTER 166

The "Forgot My Presentation" Nightmare

Scenario: You show up to an important presentation only to realize you forgot your materials.

So What?: Stay calm and improvise! You know the content, and your ability to adapt will impress everyone.

Lesson: Preparation is key, but quick thinking saves the day. Your presence is more valuable than any slides.

CHAPTER 167
The "Let's Circle Back" Loop

Scenario: You've been in meetings where "let's circle back on that" is said so many times, you feel like you're stuck in a never-ending circle. When exactly are we circling back? Nobody knows.

So What?: Sometimes "circle back" means "let's never talk about this again." Take a deep breath, and maybe sneak in a "let's square that off" for balance.

Lesson: Office lingo is a language of its own. Learn it, love it, and use it wisely.

CHAPTER 168
The "That's Not My Job" Colleague

Scenario: You need a tiny bit of help from a colleague, but their immediate response is, "That's not my job." Even if it's something they could do in 30 seconds, they make it clear they're not going to budge.

So What?: Smile, find someone else, and maybe send them a job description for reference.

Lesson: Teamwork isn't always in the job description, but the best employees know when to go beyond it.

CHAPTER 170
The One Who Forgets Your Name

Scenario: You've been working with the same colleague for over a year, yet they still can't remember your name. Every time they call you by the wrong name, it's a new adventure.

So What?: You could correct them, or you could just start responding to whatever name they give you. It's a free identity rollercoaster.

Lesson: Names are important… but sometimes it's just fun to see how far you can go before they catch on.

CHAPTER 171
The Office Group Chat Explosion

Scenario: The Office group chat starts with work topics, but by the afternoon it's become a chaotic meme fest with pet pictures, random GIFs, and someone's lunch review.

So What?: Ride the wave! Group chats are unpredictable. You'll either laugh or roll your eyes, but it's all part of the Office fun.

Lesson: Work can wait—sometimes you just need to know who has the best cat meme.

CHAPTER 172
The Professional Juggler

Scenario: One of your colleagues insists they're a "master multitasker" and spends meetings typing, talking, and texting all at once—while contributing about 10% to each task.

So What?: Sit back and watch the juggling act. They'll either drop something or magically keep everything in the air. Either way, it's quite the performance.

Lesson: Multitasking is overrated—sometimes focusing on one thing is the real superpower.

CHAPTER 173
The Over-Organized Desk

Scenario: Your colleague's desk looks like it's been curated by an interior designer—everything color-coordinated, not a single paper out of place. It's so pristine, you're afraid to breathe near it.

So What?: Admire from a distance. Just don't mess it up. For some, their workspace is a shrine to productivity.

Lesson: Everyone's got their own version of "organized." For some, it's piles of papers, for others, it's a desk that looks untouched by human hands.

CHAPTER 174
The Office Plant Obsession

Scenario: There's one person in the Office who treats their desk plants like family. They talk to them, water them religiously, and panic if anyone so much as touches a leaf.

So What?: Leave the plants alone, and maybe compliment them every now and then. After all, those plants might just be their best friends.

Lesson: Office plants are like little green therapists—they bring calm to the chaos, even if their caretaker takes it a bit too seriously.

CHAPTER 175
The Neverending Training Session

Scenario: You sit through a training session that feels like it's never going to end. The slides just keep coming, and the trainer's voice starts sounding like a lullaby.

So What?: Power through with coffee and the occasional nod of fake enthusiasm. Eventually, all training sessions end... right?

Lesson: Endurance is a skill. The real training isn't about the content—it's about staying awake.

CHAPTER 176
The Colleague with the Best Snacks

Scenario: One of your colleagues is always stocked with the best snacks—cookies, chips, candies—ready to share. It's like a mini-mart at their desk.

So What?: Make friends with them! Snack breaks are even better when someone's willing to share the goods.

Lesson: It's not just about the snacks—it's about the gesture of generosity. Sharing creates bonds, even if it's over a bag of chips.

CHAPTER 177

The Colleague Who Lights Up the Room

Scenario: There's one person in the of ice whose positivity is contagious. No matter what's going on, they make the Office a brighter, happier place.

So What?: Surround yourself with people who bring out the best in you. Their energy will inspire you to face challenges with a smile.

Lesson: Positivity is powerful. The more you spread it, the more it comes back to you.

CHAPTER 178
The Unexpected Mentor

Scenario: You start working with a colleague and realize they have a wealth of experience and wisdom to share. Without even trying, they become a mentor who helps you see things in a new light.

So What?: Sometimes the best mentors are the ones you didn't expect. Embrace their guidance, learn from their stories, and pass that knowledge along when you can.

Lesson: Great mentors don't always have the title—they're the people who lift you up when you least expect it.

CHAPTER 179
The Power of Listening

Scenario: A big project lands on your plate, but your team comes together, each person contributing their strengths to get it done.

So What?: Together, you accomplish more than you ever could alone. Celebrate each person's unique skills and the magic of collaboration.

Lesson: A strong team is unstoppable. When everyone works together, even the toughest tasks become achievable.

CHAPTER 180
The Surprising Source of Inspiration

Scenario: You hear an inspiring story from a colleague about how they overcame a tough situation, and it reignites your own motivation.

So What?: Inspiration can come from unexpected places. Stay open to it, and you'll find new sources of energy and passion when you least expect it.

Lesson: Everyone has a story that can inspire you. Keep listening, and you'll never run out of reasons to keep pushing forward.

CHAPTER 181
The Coffee Shop "Influencer"

Scenario: Your colleague takes a coffee break, but instead of quickly grabbing a cup, they spend 10 minutes snapping photos of their latte for Instagram. The rest of the Office waits impatiently for them to return... with the perfect shot.

So What?: Smile, let them live their influencer dreams, and hope they remember to bring back coffee for the rest of the team.

Lesson: For some, work-life balance means making sure every moment is Instagram-worthy—even coffee breaks.

CHAPTER 182
The Surprise Desk Gift

Scenario: You arrive at work and find a little gift on your desk—a treat or a small note of appreciation from a secret admirer (or just a thoughtful colleague).

So What?: Smile, enjoy the moment, and savor the surprise! Sometimes it's the small, unexpected gestures that make the day special.

Lesson: Thoughtful acts, big or small, can turn an ordinary day into something extraordinary. Spread kindness—it'll come back to you in the most delightful ways.

CHAPTER 183

The "One More Thing" Boss

Scenario: Just as you're about to clock out for the day, your boss swings by and says, "Oh, one more thing…" That "one more thing" turns into a full project, and suddenly, you're pulling overtime.

So What?: Take a deep breath, and maybe "forget" to check your email after 5 p.m. next time.

Lesson: "One more thing" is never just one more thing. Prepare accordingly.

CHAPTER 184
The Unplanned Office Dance Party

Scenario: Someone plays music during a break, and suddenly, the whole team is busting out dance moves in the middle of the Office.

So What?: Go with it! It's a chance to let loose and bond with colleagues in a fun, unexpected way.

Lesson: A little spontaneity can lift everyone's spirits. Sometimes, what the Office really needs is an impromptu dance break.

CHAPTER 185
The Last-Minute Team Save

Scenario: A deadline is looming, and you're behind, but your team rallies together to help you finish the project just in time.

So What?: Celebrate your amazing team! Teamwork makes the dream work, and you've got the best one around.

Lesson: You don't have to do everything alone. Leaning on your team not only strengthens the bond but also makes the impossible possible.

CHAPTER 186
The Free Office Lunch Surprise

Scenario: You sit down for lunch, and a colleague waves you over to join them for an unexpected free meal—the company's treating the whole team!

So What?: Free food is always a win. Enjoy it and use the opportunity to connect with colleagues.

Lesson: Shared meals are the glue that brings teams together. Whether planned or spontaneous, they create moments of camaraderie.

CHAPTER 187
The "Random Compliment" Day

Scenario: The office decides today is "random compliment day," and everyone goes around giving each other compliments. Suddenly, the workplace is filled with good vibes.

So What?: Embrace the positivity. Compliments are contagious, and they have the power to make the whole team feel amazing.

Lesson: Don't wait for a designated day to uplift others. Kind words are always welcome and can change the entire atmosphere of the Office.

CHAPTER 188
The Office Prank (That's Actually Fun)

Scenario: You open your drawer to find it filled with balloons—harmless, fun, and bringing laughter to the whole Office.

So What?: Laugh it off, snap a photo for posterity, and maybe start plotting your own light-hearted revenge.

Lesson: Good-natured Office pranks can break the routine and bring laughter to the workday. Just keep it friendly and fun!

CHAPTER 189
The Snow Day Surprise

Scenario: It's snowing heavily outside, and the Office decides to shut down early for a snow day. Everyone rushes out like it's elementary school all over again.

So What?: Enjoy the rare adult snow day! Whether you build a snowman or curl up with a hot drink, take advantage of the unexpected break.

Lesson: Work will always be there, but snow days are fleeting. Embrace the childlike joy of an unexpected day off.

CHAPTER 190
The Impromptu Birthday Celebration

Scenario: You come into work on your birthday, not expecting anything, but your colleagues surprise you with cake, balloons, and a card signed by the whole team.

So What?: Feel the love and enjoy the sweet moment—there's nothing like a workplace birthday surprise!

Lesson: Celebrating milestones, big or small, is what brings teams together. It's the little things that make work feel like family.

CHAPTER 191
The Friendly Office Competitions

Scenario: The office decides to hold a friendly competition—whether it's a steps challenge or a trivia quiz, suddenly everyone's getting competitive (in a fun way).

So What?: Jump in! Even if you're not winning, it's the fun of participation that counts. Plus, you might discover hidden talents.

Lesson: A little friendly competition can bring out the best in everyone. It's not about the prize; it's about the team spirit.

CHAPTER 192
The "Pay It Forward" Moment

Scenario: Someone helps you out at work without expecting anything in return, and it inspires you to pay it forward by helping a colleague in need.

So What?: Acts of kindness ripple through the Office. A little help can create a cycle of positivity.

Lesson: Workplace culture is built on small acts of kindness. The more you give, the more positivity you create.

CHAPTER 193
The Colleague Who Always Has Your Back

Scenario: When things go wrong, you can always count on one colleague to have your back, offer support, or step in when you need it most.

So What?: Appreciate the teamwork. Having someone you can rely on makes even the toughest days better.

Lesson: Trust is built over time, and when you have someone who always supports you, the workplace feels a lot more manageable.

CHAPTER 194
The "Forgot My Glasses" Presentation

Scenario: You forgot your reading glasses, and now you're squinting at your presentation like it's written in hieroglyphics. Meanwhile, the audience looks at you like they're deciphering a new language.

So What?: Squinting can be charming if you do it with confidence! Bluff your way through, or ask someone in the front row to read out loud.

Lesson: Sometimes, forgetting the small stuff makes for the best stories. Glasses or not, you're still the expert.

CHAPTER 195
The Overly Ambitious Lunch Choice

Scenario: You brought an extra-healthy quinoa salad to work because you're *trying* to be good. But halfway through eating it, you find yourself eyeing your colleague's cheeseburger like it's the last meal on earth.

So What?: Salads are for Instagram, but real life needs cheeseburgers sometimes. Next time, pack something that satisfies your soul *and* your stomach.

Lesson: Work lunches are a marathon, not a sprint. It's about balance—eat what makes you happy, not what looks impressive in the Office fridge.

CHAPTER 196
The Accidental Screen Share

Scenario: You're sharing your screen on a Zoom call, only to realize halfway through that your open tabs include a few *non-work-related* searches—like "cat memes" and "how to cook perfect lasagna."

So What?: Everyone loves a good cat meme. Own it, make a joke, and get back to the presentation. No harm done!

Lesson: Screen sharing is like walking a tightrope—always double-check before you click. But if you fall, at least it's a funny story.

CHAPTER 197
The Coffee Cup Identity Crisis

Scenario: The breakroom is full of identical coffee mugs, and now you're playing detective trying to figure out which one is yours. Did you grab Karen's cup, or is this Greg's from accounting?

So What?: Coffee is coffee. Just pick one, act casual, and if anyone catches you, say you're taste-testing the Office brews.

Lesson: Labeling your mug can save a lot of awkwardness, but in a caffeine emergency, all bets are off.

CHAPTER 198

The "Can I Pick Your Brain?" Trap

Scenario: A colleague asks to "pick your brain" for "just five minutes," but an hour later, you're knee-deep in a full-on strategy session you didn't sign up for.

So What?: Smile, nod, and gently steer the conversation back to the original topic—or keep a stopwatch handy next time!

Lesson: Brain-picking is contagious, but setting boundaries is key. You can share your brilliance without giving away the whole playbook.

CHAPTER 199
The Unexpected Promotion Celebration

Scenario: You weren't expecting a promotion, but out of the blue, you get the good news! Your colleagues throw an impromptu celebration with confetti and cheers.

So What?: Soak it in! Hard work often pays off when you least expect it, and nothing beats a surprise promotion celebration.

Lesson: Success is sweet, but sharing it with those who support you makes it even sweeter.

CHAPTER 200
The "So What?" Moment

Scenario: After countless meetings, missed deadlines, awkward office moments, and the occasional tech disaster, you find yourself reflecting on it all. The frustrations, the laughs, the chaos—none of it defined you. In fact, it made you stronger, and now you're armed with the ultimate secret weapon: the ability to laugh it off.

So What?: Work will always be a bit unpredictable. You'll spill coffee on your boss, accidentally hit "Reply All," forget a deadline, or make a fool of yourself in a meeting. But the real victory is how you bounce back. The trick isn't avoiding chaos—it's embracing it with a smile, a shrug, and a big "So what?"

Lesson: Life, like work, is full of hiccups, big and small. But here's the thing: You're resilient, resourceful, and way more equipped to handle it all than you think. When the going gets tough, laugh a little louder, roll with the punches, and keep moving forward. After all, the most successful people aren't the ones who avoid mistakes—they're the ones who turn those mistakes into stories.

The Final **So What?:** So what if you had a bad day? So what if you didn't land the promotion, missed a deadline, or made a fool of yourself in a Zoom meeting? None of those things define you. What defines you is your ability to keep cool, keep laughing, and keep going. Because when the Office chaos strikes (and it always will), you'll be ready with the perfect response: *So what?*

About the Author

Maggie has embraced each twist and turn of her professional journey with curiosity and resilience. Along the way, she discovered her true love for writing, where she now shares her insights to help others find joy and balance in their work lives.

Maggie's writing blends practical wisdom with heartfelt encouragement, inspiring readers to approach their work with confidence, purpose, and a sense of adventure. She believes that a fulfilling career isn't just about climbing the ladder but about finding happiness and meaning in every step.

When she's not writing, Maggie loves diving into a good book, playing Electone, exploring new places, and spending time with her friends, family, and beloved cats. Through her words, she hopes to uplift others and remind them that life's greatest journeys are those filled with curiosity, joy, and an open heart.

www.ingramcontent.com/pod-product-compliance
Lightning Source LLC
Chambersburg PA
CBHW071451220526
45472CB00003B/761